Paddle Steamers of the Alps

lie Brown &
McKendrick

Be. ...et, *Stadt Luzern*
dressed overall for Swiss National Day.

Front Cover: Lake Lucerne's *Schiller* arriving at Bauen.
Inside Front Cover: *Gisela* approaching Traunkirchen , on the Traunsee.
Inside Back Cover: The last operational paddle steamer on Lake Como, *Concordia* leaves Bellagio.
Back Cover: The famous *La Suisse,* of the Lake Geneva fleet, at Évian.

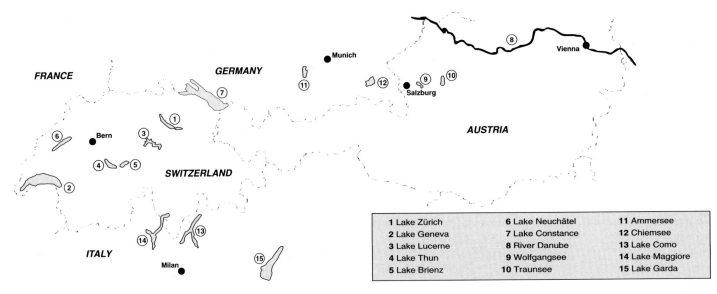

1 Lake Zürich	**6** Lake Neuchâtel	**11** Ammersee
2 Lake Geneva	**7** Lake Constance	**12** Chiemsee
3 Lake Lucerne	**8** River Danube	**13** Lake Como
4 Lake Thun	**9** Wolfgangsee	**14** Lake Maggiore
5 Lake Brienz	**10** Traunsee	**15** Lake Garda

Around the edges of the Alpine range there lies a succession of lakes, varying in size from the 45-mile-long Lake Geneva to tiny lakes just a few hundred yards across such as the deep and mysterious Kammersee in the Austrian Salzkammergut. Many of them share the feature that they penetrate into the Alps at one end only, while the other is in gently rolling hills.

This results in a combination of scenic grandeur and accessibility which has produced a flourishing tourist industry, so it is no surprise that shipping services operate on many of them. If we include the nearby River Danube we find a remarkable total of 28 paddle vessels – 17 of them still steam-powered – engaged in these sailings. The ships also vary in size, from the 256-feet-long trio on Lake Geneva and the 255-feet sisters on the Danube down to the tiny *Kaiser Franz Josef I* measuring only 110 feet.

This booklet is intended to offer a brief introduction to these vessels. Most of the areas mentioned have produced more detailed publications covering their own ships. A few vessels have been included which were formerly paddle steamers since their history is sufficiently interesting to warrant their inclusion. A brief description is given of each area of operation with an indication, where possible, of how the paddlers are deployed. Further information is available from the Tourist Offices of the various countries.

Lake Zürich is 27 miles long and between one and two miles wide. It points northwest at one end and curves gently so that it is facing east at the other. It is almost cut in two, six miles from its eastern end by a causeway carrying a road and railway, the Sudostbahn, between Rapperswil and Pfäffikon. There is, however, a narrow channel which allows ships to pass through to the upper lake (the Obersee), although they have to compete with yachts, motorboats and even swimmers. Diving off the road bridge appears to be a popular pastime, and the approach of a paddle steamer seems to add to the enjoyment.

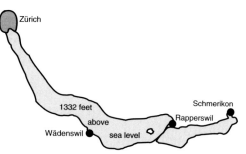

The northwestern end of the Lake is dominated by Zürich, Switzerland's largest city, and an international commercial and banking centre. Its suburbs stretch some distance along both banks of the Lake, and there is a considerable spread of population throughout its length. This gives the Lake a totally different character from all the others in Switzerland. Rather than a tourist centre, it is a recreational area for the local people, with a heavier emphasis on water sports, etc. The scenery is pleasant, but not spectacular, and it is only near the eastern end that the Alps come close to the Lake.

Shipping services are based in Zürich, and the main route is to Rapperswil. Six or seven return sailings are provided on weekdays with three extra on Sundays – again an indication of the local nature of the day excursion traffic. These sailings call at points on both sides of the Lake, and there are also supplementary services across it connecting the main villages. The Obersee has one sailing on weekdays and two on Sundays.

Lake Zürich is bordered by three cantons – the largely independent states which make up the Swiss Confederation. In addition to Canton Zürich, where the steamers are based, there are also the cantons of Schwyz and St. Gallen. The steamers fly the flags of these last two as courtesy flags when visiting "foreign" ports.

The paddle steamers operate one sailing to Rapperswil and one to Wädenswil daily, and also one sailing running the entire length of the Lake from Zürich to Schmerikon and back on Sundays and Wednesdays. This results in both steamers being in commission on two days a week in July and August, and it is worth timing a visit to Lake Zürich to include this. In addition some special sailings and evening cruises are operated, but these are only advertised locally.

Stadt Zürich heads for the narrow channel which allows access to the Obersee.

STADT ZÜRICH

Builders:	Escher-Wyss, Zürich
Launched:	8th May 1909
Length:	194 feet
Displacement:	291 tonnes
Speed:	14·6 knots
Passengers:	850

Because of their different utilisation, the Lake Zürich steamers are fitted out on a less lavish scale than those on the other lakes. They are still very pleasant to travel on, with an abundance of open deck space and first-rate catering services.

Stadt Zürich was thoroughly renovated in 1980, and reboiled in 1990. In 1981 she was fitted with a telescopic funnel and hinged mast to enable her to pass under the road and rail bridge near Rapperswil and enter the Obersee, which she had been previously unable to do. It must be quite unusual for an inland lake steamer to have a new section of lake made available to her after more than 70 years in service.

STADT RAPPERSWIL

Builders:	Escher-Wyss, Zürich
Launched:	16th March 1914
Length:	194 feet
Displacement:	282.5 tonnes
Speed:	14·6 knots
Passengers:	850

Stadt Rapperswil is a sister-ship of *Stadt Zürich*, but there are two small points which distinguish them. Most obviously, *Stadt Rapperswil* has an enormous yardarm on her mast which *Stadt Zürich* lacks, and also she has five broad vents in her paddlebox as opposed to the latter's more numerous small vents.

The announcement of the intended withdrawal of *Stadt Rapperswil* in 1971 caused a storm of protest in the Zürich area. Public opinion was mobilised in the ship's favour, and she was extensively renovated in 1972. She was reboiled in 1985/86. Like her sister, she was given a telescopic funnel and hinged mast to allow her to sail into the Obersee.

Lake Geneva – Lac Léman in French and Genfersee in German – is the largest of the Alpine lakes, 45 miles long and 8·5 miles across at its widest. Because of its size it can get quite rough in a strong wind – the nearest to open sea sailing that it is possible to experience in Switzerland. Most of the southern shore is in France, and it is necessary to carry a passport when travelling from one country to the other.

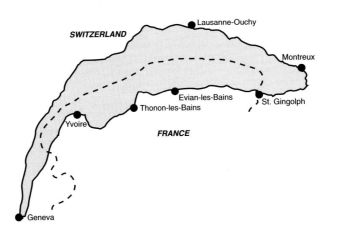

Shipping services are operated by the Compagnie Générale de Navigation sur le Lac Léman, or CGN, which is based in Ouchy, the port of Lausanne. The ships therefore fly the Swiss ensign, but they also fly the French tricolor at the bow.

The cosmopolitan city of Geneva is the main attraction at the western end of the Lake. With broad avenues, lakeside promenades and fine shops, its opulence stems from its long-held position as a neutral headquarters for international organisations, both political and commercial. Not far from the city centre, on the lakeside, stands the Palais des Nations, built as the headquarters of the League of Nations, and now used by some organisations which are part of the United Nations. A notable feature of the harbour is the Jet d'Eau, a 500-foot high column of water. This end of the Lake is not mountainous, but the pure white cone of the peak of Mont Blanc can be seen in the distance.

Low hills border the Lake for most of its length, with terraced vineyards covering much of the Swiss side, but towards the eastern end, from Montreux onwards, some of the snow-covered summits of the High Alps are visible. Another point of interest near Montreux is the Castle of Chillon, immortalised in a poem by Byron.

Only two return sailings each day run the entire length of the Lake between Geneva and St. Gingolph or vice versa, but there are cruises round the section near Geneva marketed as the Tour du Petit Lac, and more frequently round the more scenic Montreux end known as the Tour du Haut Lac. Most services radiate from the main base at Lausanne-Ouchy, especially to Évian, the main resort on the French shore, with some sailings extended to Thonon and Yvoire, a beautifully preserved mediæval village.

Between 1933 and 1960 five of the oldest paddle steamers were converted to diesel-electric propulsion, but then there was a change in Company policy, and four of the five remaining steamers were renovated and reboilered. There followed a reversion in favour of diesel-electric drive, so that the remaining steamer, *Helvétie*, lost her unusual "Uniflow" engine and was fitted with a second-hand replacement. With all the older units now having received attention, the future of the paddlers seems secure.

forward of the paddle shaft and the engines abaft – an unusual arrangement for a Continental steamer. She also has larger windows round the forward end of the observation saloon than her sisters.

As with all Swiss steamers, her first-class saloon *(below)* is most attractively fitted out. In this case it is in neo-classic "Louis XVI" style. She was thoroughly renovated and reboilered in 1970.

She normally provides the lunchtime cruise from Lausanne to Évian and back, and then cruises round the eastern half of the Lake via Évian, Montreux and Vevey – the "Tour du Haut Lac".

LA SUISSE

Builders:	Sulzer Bros., Winterthur
Entered Service:	25th May 1910
Length overall:	256 feet
Displacement:	461 tonnes
Speed:	15·6 knots
Passengers:	1400

La Suisse was the first of the three large paddlers on Lake Geneva, and was the flagship of the fleet for her first 80 years. She is different in appearance from the other two, as she has her boiler

SAVOIE

Builders:	Sulzer Bros., Winterthur
Entered service:	23rd May 1914
Length overall:	217 feet
Displacement:	367 tonnes
Speed:	14·8 knots
Passengers:	1000

Like *La Suisse*, *Savoie* also has her boiler and funnel forward of the paddle shaft, and the engine abaft, so that the engine is "pushing" the ship. Being one of the smaller and more economical of the steam ships, she was used for winter services until the conversion of some of the other paddlers to diesel drive. She also has a saloon in Louis XVI style, but it has lost some of its character due to alterations.

She was laid up in 1962 with boiler defects, but in 1966-67 she was reboilered and thoroughly renovated at a cost of more than one million francs.

A lunch-time cruise from Lausanne across to the French village of Yvoire, followed by a tour of the "Haut Lac" – in the opposite direction to that of *La Suisse* – is her normal employment.

SIMPLON

Builders:	Sulzer Bros., Winterthur
Built:	1914 – 1920
Length overall:	256 feet
Displacement:	483 tonnes
Speed:	15·9 knots
Passengers:	1500

Simplon, a near-sister of *La Suisse*, has the distinction of being the largest ship on the Swiss Lakes, indeed she is the largest steamship there has ever been in Switzerland. Likewise, her 1400 hp engine, along with that of *La Suisse* and *Helvétie*'s original engine, are the most powerful steam engines ever built for Swiss steamers.

Simplon was ordered in 1914 but due to the intervention of the Great War and its effect on tourism, she was not completed until 1920.

Her first-class saloon is particularly fine, and her spaciousness and excellent facilities make her a popular choice for charters and special sailings. She rarely appears on scheduled sailings.

When she was reboilered in 1968, she was fitted with two small boilers in place of the larger original one, and her fuel consumption now compares unfavourably with *La Suisse* which still has a single large boiler.

RHÔNE

Builders:	Sulzer Bros., Winterthur
Entered service:	1927
Length overall:	215 feet
Displacement:	364 tonnes
Speed:	14·8 knots
Passengers:	950

Rhône was the last Swiss-built paddle steamer. She was ordered as a replacement for the *Bonivard* of 1898 which had been destroyed by fire in 1925.

Her compound diagonal engine has hydraulically-driven valves, so that there are no eccentrics. It also has automatic lubrication which results in the cranks being enclosed. She was reboiled in 1969.

Her normal employment in the off-peak season is the 0915 sailing from Geneva, which covers the full length of the lake to St. Gingolph and back – a journey of just under 12 hours, but in July and August she operates short cruises from Geneva. She has for many years been the steamer with the greatest annual mileage.

MONTREUX

Builders:	Sulzer Bros., Winterthur
Entered service:	1904
Converted :	1959/60
Length overall:	218 feet
Displacement:	323 tonnes
Speed:	15·6 knots
Passengers:	1000

Montreux sailed as a steam paddler until 1958. Diesel-electric drive then replaced the steam engine, and she re-entered service in 1961. She was given a distinctive modern funnel with company crests on the sides, but in 1986 this was replaced by a funnel of similar design to those of the remaining steamers. To begin with, the lower part was painted white, but three years later it became yellow.

She is normally in commission for about half of the year, and her number of days in service is usually second only to *Italie* or *Vevey*.

VEVEY

Builders:	Sulzer Bros., Winterthur
Entered service:	1907
Converted:	1954/55
Length overall:	210 feet
Displacement:	268 tonnes
Speed:	15·4 knots
Passengers:	900

The earliest diesel-electric conversion still in operation, *Vevey*, had her steam engine removed in 1954. She and her sister-ship *Italie* are very economical to run, and have sometimes been used to maintain winter services, although the appearance of the new motorship *Léman* in 1991 has largely put a stop to this .

Her modern funnel, fitted at the time of conversion, was in 1987 replaced by one of more traditional design, but more raked than *Montreux*'s, and it was also restored to yellow with black top in 1989. The photographs show her with old and with new funnels.

ITALIE

Builders:	Sulzer Bros., Winterthur
Entered service:	1908
Converted:	1956/58
Length overall:	210 feet
Displacement:	263 tonnes
Speed:	15·4 knots
Passengers:	900

Italie and her sister *Vevey* have each travelled more than two million kilometres (1·25 million miles), and *Italie* often achieves the highest annual mileage of all the Swiss paddlers. This is not surprising, as her normal run has been for many years the 0850 from St. Gingolph to Geneva and back, thus traversing the entire length of the Lake twice every day. In addition, she has regular Wednesday evening "Dancing Boat" cruises from Montreux.

As with the other conversions of that period, the diesel engines are very well insulated, and there is little intrusion of noise or vibration into the passenger space.

HELVÉTIE

Builders:	Sulzer Bros., Winterthur
Entered service:	1926
Converted:	1975/77
Length overall:	256 feet
Displacement:	468 tonnes
Speed:	originally 16·2 knots
Passengers:	1400

When *Helvétie* was converted to diesel-electric drive in 1975-77, she lost her three-cylinder "Uniflow" engine similar to that supplied by Sulzer to *Stadt Luzern* in 1929. Her replacement machinery was second-hand, having previously powered the tug *Goliath* on the Danube. This transplant seems not to have been entirely satisfactory, and *Helvétie* is used much less than the other diesel paddlers. Most of the time she is the reserve ship at Geneva, and her principal employment is occasional evening cruises and charters. Unlike the others, her appearance was not altered when she was converted. She is most easily distinguished from her sisters *La Suisse* and *Simplon* by having decorations on the bow.

GENÈVE

In 1932 the boiler of the *Genève* of 1896 was in need of replacement. Six years earlier, a side-wheel ferry on the Ohio River had been successfully converted to diesel-electric drive, and this mode of propulsion was also adopted for the rejuvenated *Genève*. She thus became the first diesel-electric paddler in Europe two years before the Clyde's *Talisman* was built. *Genève*, however, has her electric motor geared to the paddle shaft, whereas *Talisman* was unique with her direct drive.

Genève was so successful after her transplant that five others were similarly treated over the next 44 years. She was withdrawn in 1973 and became an accommodation ship in Geneva for the Carrefour organisation which cares for society dropouts. Once a year, *Genève* sails under her own power across Geneva harbour to berth at Paquis because her normal berth is used for a festival. In October 1992 she sailed under her own power to the CGN shipyard at Lausanne for hull repairs and painting.

VALAIS

Valais, built in 1913 is a sister-ship of *Savoie*, but on being withdrawn with boiler trouble in 1962 she was not repaired. Instead, her engine and boilers were removed, and she is now moored at the Jardin Anglais in Geneva as an office and restaurant ship.

Above right: *Genève* alongside *Helvétie* at Paquis Quay in July 1988. (Photo: Elisabeth Emmenegger)

Lake Lucerne is situated right in the centre of Switzerland and has excellent communications with the rest of the country. Its proper title is the Vierwaldstättersee – the Lake of the Four Forest Cantons. The original Swiss Confederation was founded in this area when the cantons of Schwyz, Uri and Unterwalden formed an alliance in 1291. This was confirmed at a ceremony on the Rütli meadow on 1st August 1307. Rütli is therefore a focus for Swiss patriotism, and 1st August is still a national holiday which is celebrated with great enthusiasm. The fourth lakeside canton, Luzern, joined the others in 1332.

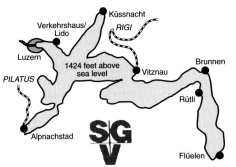

Steamer traffic on the Lake began in 1837 to provide easier access to the Gotthard Pass, one of the principal routes between northern Europe and Italy. Through steamer traffic declined when the Gotthard Railway opened in 1882, but by this time the scenic attractions of the area were beginning to be appreciated by tourists. Queen Victoria stayed in Luzern in 1868, and is reported to have climbed Mount Pilatus on a mule. Access to the mountains was made easier by the construction of Europe's first rack-and-pinion railway from Vitznau to the summit of Rigi in 1871, and others soon followed. A later development was the provision of cable cars and chairlifts to even more inaccessible peaks, and there is now a wide variety of these within easy reach of the Lake.

A further boost to tourism in the area is provided by the William Tell legend. The scene of the famous apple incident was the village of Altdorf, a short bus journey from Flüelen and well worth a visit. The legend was given worldwide publicity by the play written by the German dramatist Friedrich von Schiller – hence the names bestowed on the sister-ships of 1906/08.

The main steamer route on the Lake, with calls at most of the intermediate piers, is still the 23 miles from Luzern to Flüelen at the foot of the Gotthard Pass. In summer there are seven sailings each way for the full length of the Lake, with additional shorter runs. The long runs are normally taken by the paddle steamers and large motor vessels.

The next route in importance is that to Alpnachstad from which the world's steepest rack-and-pinion railway climbs to the summit of Pilatus – a most spectacular journey. The entrance to the arm of the lake leading this way, the Alpnachersee, is very narrow, and in 1961 the elderly swing bridge spanning the entrance was replaced by a new road and rail bridge leaving a clearance of only 25 feet. Two of the paddle steamers and all the motor vessels, except for the almost new *Schwyz* of 1959, were altered, and all subsequent ships have been built within this limit.

The third route is to Küssnacht, but since all the places in this part of the Lake can be reached by road, and some by rail, there are only three return trips per day. A small motor vessel operates the remaining route – a ferry service round the Bay of Luzern.

Sailings are fewer in spring and autumn, and there is a very restricted service on the main part of the Lake in winter. The most intensive programme of sailings, using all the paddlers, is operated in July and August, although they also sail to a lesser extent in early and late season, especially on Sundays. A motorship is sometimes substituted in very bad weather.

URI

Builders:	Sulzer Bros., Winterthur
Launched:	19th January 1901
Entered Service:	8th May 1901
Length overall:	203 feet
Displacement:	294 tonnes
Trial speed:	15·2 knots
Passengers:	800

Uri has a truly remarkable first-class saloon, with an abundance of neo-baroque carving and, since 1993, a magnificent hand-painted deckhead. In 1931 she was in collision with a cargo vessel and as a result lost the decoration on her bows. She sailed in this condition for the next 50 years, but during her major renovation in 1981 she was fitted with elegant new bow scrolls.

Before the 1961 season, because of the new road and rail bridge across the entrance to the Alpnachersee, she was given collapsible masts and funnel, and her wheelhouse was rebuilt so that it could sink by nearly four feet. This resulted in the fitting of a large aluminium canopy over the top deck. In this condition she was often used on the Alpnachstad service, but she also appeared in other parts of the Lake.

After the 1991 season Uri was taken out of service for two seasons for what amounted to a complete rebuild. This restored her to something very close to her original condition, looking like a slightly smaller version of Schiller. In the process she lost her telescopic masts and funnel, and so is now unable to go to Alpnachstad.

With 1·7 million kilometres behind her, Uri is the furthest travelled of all the remaining Swiss steamers although some of the Lake Geneva diesel paddlers have exceeded 2 million kilometres.

UNTERWALDEN

Builders:	Escher-Wyss, Zürich
Launched:	12th November 1901
Entered service:	18th May 1902
Length overall:	203 feet
Displacement:	294 tonnes
Trial speed:	14·8 knots
Passengers:	800

Unterwalden was built to the same specification as *Uri*, but by a different shipyard. She appeared a year later than her sister because her engines were on display at the Paris Exhibition of 1900. Her first-class saloon has magnificent neo-rococo carving. Like *Uri* she was altered in 1961 so that she could pass under the Acheregg bridge.

She was withdrawn after the 1977 season, and it was not until 1982 that the decision was taken to renovate her at a cost of £1·5million, much of which was raised by the Steamer Friends. A very thorough job was made of her restoration during 1983 and 1984, and she re-entered service on 16th May 1985.

She has now been given an enclosed restaurant on the upper deck, and often sails on special excursions, charters and evening cruises. She has also sometimes been used as part of the prestigious "Wilhelm Tell Express" excursion. Since 1992 she has normally given one sailing each weekday to Alpnachstad, as she is now the only paddle steamer able to do so.

Right: Unterwalden under restoration in August 1984

SCHILLER

Builders:	Sulzer Bros., Winterthur
Launched:	17th February 1906
Entered service:	21st May 1906
Length overall:	207 feet
Displacement:	320 tonnes
Trial speed:	15·4 knots
Passengers:	900

Schiller has possibly the most elegant lines of all the Swiss steamers. Her first-class saloon is in a striking "geometrical" style, with lines of dark wood on a lighter wood panelling, and inlaid designs in mother-of-pearl. Another characteristic of the ship is the vase of flowers on the main engine entablature!

After a number of years as the Cinderella of the fleet, seeing fewer days in operation than the others, *Schiller* was taken out of service in 1976 for a very thorough renovation, and has now regained her place as one of the premier vessels. Her normal employment is a return trip on the main route from Luzern to Flüelen, but a recent development has been to use her on the morning run to Küssnacht on a few Sundays each summer, much to the delight of enthusiasts.

Winter scene at the SGV shipyard (Photo: Mario Gavazzi)

GALLIA

Builders:	Escher-Wyss, Zürich
Launched:	2nd June 1913
Entered service:	10th July 1913
Length overall:	206 feet
Displacement:	325 tonnes
Trial speed:	17·2 knots
Passengers:	850

Gallia has a less ornate interior than her older sisters, but her chief claim to fame is her speed. She is the fastest paddle steamer on any lake in Europe, although in her normal service she does not require to show her paces. Like *Schiller*, one return trip between Luzern and Flüelen is her normal employment, and she is a popular choice for charters.

She was withdrawn for the whole of the 1977 season for a complete renovation, and on her return to service a further trial run showed that her facility for speed was unimpaired despite her 64 years.

STADT LUZERN

Builders:	Sachsenberg Bros, Rosslau-on-Elbe, Germany
Engines built by:	Sulzer Bros., Winterthur
Launched:	14th December 1927
Entered service:	24th June 1928
Re-entered service:	5th July 1929
Length overall:	208 feet
Displacement:	410·5 tonnes
Trial speed:	14·2 knots
Passengers:	1200

Amid much local protest, the order for *Stadt Luzern* went to Germany. On one of her trial runs she broke down and had to be towed back to the Company's shipyard. On her first day in service, cracks appeared in several places in the engine, and it had to be completely replaced. Sulzer Brothers supplied a three-crank "Uniflow" engine, and as a penalty Sachsenberg had to build the hull of the small motor vessel *Rütli*. The Uniflow engine has hydraulic gearing and therefore no eccentric valve gear. It also has automatic lubrication, and so the cranks are enclosed. Some years ago the original metal covers were replaced by transparent ones, and the engine can now be seen by the public.

On 25th July 1940, General Guisan, Commander-in-Chief of the Swiss army, and his senior officers travelled on *Stadt Luzern* to Rütli for a historic meeting to decide on Switzerland's position in World War II. A plaque on board *(inset)* commemorates this event. Another big occasion for *Stadt Luzern* was when Queen Elizabeth and Prince Philip sailed on her to Rütli during their state visit to Switzerland in 1980.

During the winters of 1987-89, *Stadt Luzern* has had a very thorough renovation, although the only external evidence is that her top deck restaurant has been extended by about 15 feet.

Stadt Luzern was built as flagship of the fleet, a position she has held ever since. She is almost invariably on the 1130 sailing from Luzern to Flüelen and back, as her larger capacity is often required on what is usually the busiest run of the day.

BIEBO (ex STADT LUZERN)

Stadt Luzern was the first paddle steamer on the Lake, where she served as a passenger vessel for 35 years. In 1872 she was taken out of service and converted to carry cargo only. She was not used much in this form, and in 1881 had her superstructure removed, after which she was used for towing. Seven years later she was fitted with a small vertical 2-cylinder steam engine and screw propeller. After a major overhaul in 1903 she became the bunker ship for the fleet. Her steam engine was superseded by an oil motor in 1924, and this in turn gave way to a diesel engine in 1966.

By 1967 there were no coal-fired ships in regular service, and she was again converted, this time to treat bilge water from the rest of the fleet. In this rôle she continues to this day, bearing the name BIEBO (BIlgenwasser-EntleerungsBOot).

PFAHLRAMME (ex ST. GOTTHARD)

St Gotthard was the second paddle steamer on the Lake, and sailed on passenger service from 1843 until 1872, including a spell as a troopship in the civil war of 1845. Like *Stadt Luzern*, she was converted to carry cargo, and for a time transported building materials for the Gotthard Railway. In 1891 she was converted to become a floating piledriver, since the steamship company owns the landing stages, and she has fulfilled this purpose for over a century.

She was given a second hand steam engine and propeller in 1898, and this served until 1973/4, when a diesel engine replaced the steam one. The pile-driving equipment remained steam-powered until 1988, but even that submitted to the ubiquitous diesel during a modernisation programme. In winter she still goes round the Lake repairing the landing stages, but in summer she is

usually to be seen at the SGV yard in Luzern.

It will be noticed that the life span of the first two paddlers as passenger ships was very short by Swiss Lake standards. This was mainly due to the rapidly improving standards of comfort expected by the growing number of tourists.

Pfahlramme and *Biebo* on 31st July 1987 – the latter's 150th birthday.

Stadt Luzern (I) on a special issue of stamps in 1987 to commemorate 150 years of steam power on Lake Lucerne.

WALDSTÄTTER (ex RHEIN, ex BEN JONSON)

This far-travelled vessel was built as P.S. *Ben Jonson* for the L.C.C. Thames service inaugurated in 1905. When this service closed in 1907 the fleet was sold, and *Ben Jonson* was bought by the Lake Lucerne company for £1100. She left London under tow on 27th September 1909 and, after crossing the North Sea, was taken up the Rhine to Duisburg. From there she sailed under her own power to Basel, arriving on 16th October. She was then cut into sections and taken overland to Luzern. After reassembly, and with a new superstructure, she entered service as P.S. *Rhein* on 23rd March 1911.

Because of her fairly high fuel consumption, she was not much used after 1918, and was finally withdrawn from service in 1939. Over the next five years, as she was partly dismantled, the hull was found to be in good condition, so in 1944, with the wartime shortage of steel, it was decided to rebuild her into a motorship. She was lengthened from 139 to 164 feet, and as *Waldstätter* she entered service on 2nd February 1949. In her third incarnation she has at last been highly successful and continues to be used on all routes, summer and winter.

Sadly, this historic ship is unlikely to remain in service after 1994.

WILHELM TELL

Wilhelm Tell was built by Sulzer in 1908 as a sister ship to *Schiller*, although some small details make her profile marginally less attractive. She gave 62 years of faithful service with almost no external alteration to her appearance except for the construction of a wheelhouse about 1920. In 1961 she was given the top section of funnel which had been removed from *Uri* during her alterations. It is noticeably narrower than the others in the fleet.

The announcement of the withdrawal of *Wilhelm Tell* in 1970 prompted the founding of the preservation movement in Luzern. The campaign was unsuccessful in keeping her in service, but it did secure the future of the remaining steamers.

Wilhelm Tell is now a very pleasant floating restaurant at the Luzern promenade.

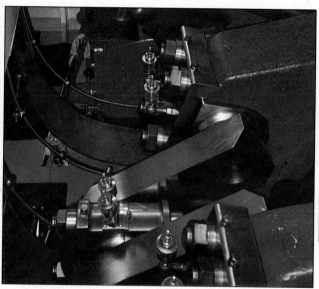

Left: Climax of the Swiss National Day celebrations is the evening fireworks cruise from Luzern. *Schiller, Gallia, Unterwalden* and *Uri* are lined up ready for the prompt departure at 8.00 p.m. This page: "*Schiller* is perfect!"

Above left: Engines

Above right: Detail of dining saloon panel, showing mother-of-pearl inlays.

Right: Leaving Treib, with the twin peaks of the Mythen in the background.

RIGI

Rigi's hull and engine were built in London by Ditchborne & Mare and Penn & Son respectively. In contrast to the first two steamers on the lake, *Rigi*, the fourth steamer was a passenger vessel for 104 years. She was not used, however, in the years 1915-20, and in 1921 there were plans to convert her to diesel, but these came to nothing. In 1958 she was taken on a low-loader through the streets of Luzern to the Swiss Museum of Transport, then under construction, where she was given the place of honour as the centrepiece. She is used as a restaurant, and her oscillating engine (not the original but a replacement fitted in 1894) can be turned by an electric motor.

THE SWISS MUSEUM OF TRANSPORT (Verkehrshaus)

The Transport Museum is situated about a mile from the centre of Luzern, along the north shore of the Lake. It can be reached in about 5 minutes by trolleybus (route No.2) or in 11 minutes by steamer.

Opened in 1959, it has gradually been extended and now occupies 12 buildings. It is considered by many to be the finest Transport Museum in Europe, perhaps in the world. The centrepiece is the paddle steamer *Rigi* of 1848, and there are over 60 locomotives, 40 cars and 35 aircraft. There are also imaginative displays covering post and telecommunications, space travel and tourism.

The most impressive exhibit in the Ship Hall consists of the boilers, main engine and starboard paddle wheel of the 1895 *Pilatus* – see the illustration on the right. The engine and wheel are turned by an electric motor. Several floors of this building are

taken up by nautical exhibits, with many ship models including one of *Waverley*. A visit to the Museum is a "must" for anyone with an interest in any form of transport.

The principal resort in the Bernese Oberland is Interlaken which, as its name suggests, lies between two lakes – Brienz to the east and Thun to the west. The river Aare, flowing westwards, falls by several feet, and the two lakes are therefore completely separate as far as shipping is concerned. The services, however, are operated on both lakes by the Bern-Lötschberg-Simplon Railway (BLS).

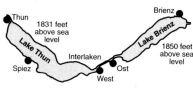

Lake Thun is the larger of the two, being about 12 miles by 2 miles. The BLS runs a very intensive service with modern motorships. The last operating paddle steamer on the lake, *Blümlisalp*, was withdrawn in 1971, and languished for nearly 20 years while one plan after another was made for her future. In 1988 it was decided to restore her to active service, and the photographs below show her restoration taking place in a dry berth in the Kander Delta. Four years later she returned to service,

giving one return trip daily except Mondays from Thun to Interlaken, and weekly evening cruises in the height of the season.

Measuring about 10 miles by 2 miles, Lake Brienz is the smallest Swiss lake still to have an operational paddle steamer. It is hemmed in by mountains which are not particularly high, but on the southern shore they drop steeply into the water. There is a spectacular waterfall at Giessbach. Other lakeside attractions include the Brienzer Rothorn Railway, which is mainly steam-operated, and the open-air Swiss Folklore Museum at Ballenberg, near Brienz. One small point of interest is that the first steamer on the lake, the *Giessbach* introduced in 1839, was captained by one Mr Croll, a nephew of Sir Walter Scott.

Nine services run the full length of the Lake in summer, two of them operated by the paddle steamer *Lötschberg*.

Major surgery for Lake Thun's *BLÜMLISALP*. (Photos: Mario Gavazzi)

BLÜMLISALP

Builders:	Escher-Wyss, Zürich
Entered service:	1906
Withdrawn:	1971
Re-entered service:	1992
Length:	formerly 198 feet (since 1990) 206 feet
Displacement:	294 tonnes
Passengers:	1000

Blümlisalp is slightly larger than her sister *Lötschberg* on nearby Lake Brienz, but they were built by the same shipyard for the same company. One distinctive feature of the Bernese Oberland paddlers is the single large ventilator behind the bridge, instead of the usual pair. The terminal at Interlaken West is reached by a canal nearly two miles long, so *Blümlisalp* was designed for passing down the canal stern-first. The single ventilator does not obstruct the view aft while she is doing this, and she has a large bow rudder to assist with the manœuvre. The landing stage at Thun is also reached by sailing stern first down the River Aare.

For some time after her withdrawal she lay neglected, but then plans were made to include her, or part of her, in a "Vaporama" museum at Thun. However, it was eventually decided to restore her for further service. Reconstruction included reboiling and lengthening by almost 8 feet. She returned to service on 22nd May 1992, and has since proved a great attraction. In 1993 she raced the motorship *Jungfrau*, acknowledged as the fastest of the motor vessels, and beat her convincingly, regaining the "Blue Riband" of the Lake which she had lost to *Jungfrau* in 1954.

LÖTSCHBERG

Builders:	Escher-Wyss, Zürich
Entered service:	25th July 1914
Length:	182 feet
Displacement:	260 tonnes
Speed:	13·5 knots
Passengers:	900

Lötschberg entered service just a fortnight before the outbreak of the Great War, which immediately killed off the Swiss tourist industry. She was laid up for the duration of the War, but meanwhile, in 1916, the Brünig Railway from Luzern to Interlaken had been completed. Since its route ran along the whole of the north shore of the Lake, this was a further blow to the potential traffic for *Lötschberg*.

However, she re-entered service in 1919 and ran successfully until the 1970's, when her announced withdrawal sparked off the same kind of storm of public opinion as had already happened with *Wilhelm Tell* and *Stadt Rapperswil*. As a result, she was given an extensive renovation in 1974-75.

Lötschberg's terminal at Interlaken Ost is some distance downriver from the Lake, and she has to approach it stern-first. She also crosses from Ringgenberg to Bönigen stern-first on her outward journey. Consequently, like her sister on the neighbouring Lake Thun, she has a single boiler-room ventilator and a bow rudder.

In 1979 she lost her distinctive cream and white livery when she was repainted white with black and red edgings. Before the 1989 season she had a thorough renovation, which included extending the aluminium canopy on her top deck.

NEUCHÂTEL

This small paddle steamer was built in 1912 by Escher-Wyss and sailed until 1969. After her withdrawal *Neuchâtel* was converted for restaurant use and moored in her home port, Neuchâtel. She has been given a large covered restaurant on the top deck, but much of her character has been retained. Less fortunate is her sister *Fribourg* (1913-65), which has become a restaurant at Portalban. She has been more drastically altered and moved about half a mile "inland" from the Lake.

SWISS STEAMER STATISTICS

Each year the Swiss steamer operators publish the mileage recorded by each of their steamers, and their number of days in service. This information is given below for 1990, a fairly typical year.

	Miles	Days	Miles to '90
LAKE LUCERNE			
URI	4756	93	1,061,505
UNTERWALDEN	9431	146	912,763
SCHILLER	4864	80	712,947
GALLIA	4569	75	643,363
STADT LUZERN	10908	168	368,003
LAKE BRIENZ			
LÖTSCHBERG	5996	122	282,356

	Miles	Days	Miles to '90
LAKE GENEVA			
LA SUISSE	7804	120	796,739
SAVOIE	10906	106	997,637
SIMPLON	3383	52	567,257
RHÔNE	16230	129	573,034
LAKE ZÜRICH			
STADT ZÜRICH	3651	60	331,258
STADT RAPPERSWIL	4588	73	332,014

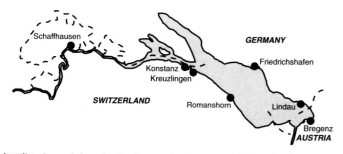

This large lake, the Bodensee in German, is 40 miles by 8 miles, and has three countries bordering it – Austria, Germany and Switzerland. Each has its own fleet on the Lake, operated by its own national railway company. Paddle steamer services came to an end in the 1960's, but one of the German paddlers, *Hohentwiel*, was used as a boat club's headquarters in the Austrian resort of Bregenz. Scheduled services are operated by motorships, many of them dating from the 1920's and 1930's. Some of the Austrian and German ships were among the first in the world to have Voith Schneider propulsion.

A Swiss company which operates from Kreuzlingen down the river Rhine as far as Schaffhausen withdrew its last paddle steamer *Schaffhausen* (1913) as recently as 1967. The service is now run by modern motorships which are designed to pass under the very low bridges across the river. Despite this, the service is sometimes disrupted by very high or very low water levels in the river. Another Swiss company runs small motorships from Rorschach a short distance up the Upper Rhine to Rheineck.

Below: 8th February 1990 – *Hohentwiel* on trials following her restoration. (Photo: Mario Gavazzi)

HOHENTWIEL

Builders:	Escher-Wyss, Zürich
Entered service:	1913
Withdrawn:	1962
Re-entered service:	1990
Length:	187 feet
Displacement:	378 tonnes

ship, and, following a very extensive rebuilding, she steamed again in 1990. She had had some additions made to her superstructure during the 1930's, but she has now been restored to her original condition. The restoration is of a particularly high standard, especially the woodwork.

She is kept very busy operating a programme of special cruises, many of them charters, from a wide variety of ports around the Lake, regularly visiting all three countries.

Hohentwiel was built in 1913 for the Royal Württemberg Steamship Company, and came under the ownership of German Railways seven years later. For most of her career she was based in Friedrichshafen. During the night of 24th April 1944 there was a severe air-raid on her home port which sank two of her sister-ships, but having been forewarned while in Konstanz she remained there and was undamaged.

She was withdrawn after the 1962 season following an engine breakdown, and sold to Bregenz Sailing Club for use as a club-house. An international society was formed in 1982 to restore the

The Danube (Donau in German) is the second-longest river in Europe, its 1740-mile length being exceeded only by the Volga. Like many great European rivers, it is still a very busy waterway, with numerous barges which are more often pushed than pulled nowadays. Much of the traffic is conveyed by vessels from East European countries, especially Russia and Romania. In addition to local excursions, cruise ships run from Vienna to the Black Sea and there is a hydrofoil service between Vienna and Budapest.

Steamship services began in 1829 when the Englishmen Andrews and Pritchard founded the First Danube Steamship Company (D.D.S.G.) which still operates the paddlers detailed below. At its height, before the turn of the century, the D.D.S.G. owned 188 steamships, including tugs, and 750 barges. Both World Wars were catastrophic for the Company, with many vessels sunk or badly damaged and many others seized as reparations. The dismembering of the Austrian Empire after 1918 greatly reduced the Company's sphere of operation, and now its passenger services are confined to the stretch between Vienna and the German border town

of Passau, although there are still considerable towing operations.

The scenery viewed from the deck of the steamer is very varied. The large towns have industrial areas along the river banks, but for most of its length the river passes through a rural setting. The Wachau valley, between Melk and Krems, is a steep-sided gorge with terraced vineyards and ruined castles – a very scenic stretch which is understandably popular with tourists. Several hydro-electric barrages have now been built across the river, and the ships have to by-pass these by negotiating sets of locks.

For the past few years the distribution of paddle vessels has been varied, although *Stadt Passau* has concentrated on the Passau-Linz section while *Stadt Wien* has performed short cruises from Vienna. The steamer *Schönbrunn* was tried on various excursion programmes in recent years, but these failed to produce sufficient patronage, and she was then sent under charter to Budapest where she served as a floating casino.

One former DDSG paddle steamer remains in a static role, appropriately named *Johann Strauss*.

JOHANN STRAUSS

Builders:	(hull ex GREIN, ex CARL LUDWIG – 1853) D.D.S.G. Yard, Budapest
	(machinery & superstructure ex JOHANN STRAUSS, ex ERZHERZOG FRANZ FERDINAND – 1913) Sachsenberg Bros.
Reconstructed:	1950
Withdrawn:	1972
Length:	230 feet

P.S. *Carl Ludwig* was one of three sister ships built in 1853, and she was renamed *Grein* in 1938. *Erzherzog* (i.e., Archduke) *Franz Ferdinand* appeared in 1913 and served as a hospital ship in the First World War. She was renamed *Johann Strauss* and was sunk by bombing at Linz in 1945. The wreck was raised and in 1950 her machinery was fitted to the hull of the *Grein*, the resulting composite ship being given the name *Johann Strauss*. After withdrawal in 1972, she served as a restaurant at Regensburg (West Germany) from 1980 till 1985, when she was returned to the Austrian capital. She is now a popular cafe in the Donaukanal in Vienna.

SCHÖNBRUNN

Builders:	D.D.S.G. Yard, Budapest
Entered service:	1912
Length:	245 feet
Displacement:	556 tonnes
Speed:	13·5 knots
Passengers:	1400 (38 in cabins)

Schönbrunn was one of three sister-ships, but *Wien* sank in 1936 following a collision with a bridge, and *Budapest* was withdrawn in 1967 and later scrapped in Greece. Following modernisation, *Schönbrunn* returned to service in 1954, post-war sailings having resumed four years earlier. She was extensively modernised in 1975.

Because of the many low bridges over the Danube, *Schönbrunn* has a hinged mast – which unfortunately seems to be kept in the "down" position for most of the time – and her funnel is mounted on a pivot. It has large counterweights and is operated by wires from the engine room. Her engine room is more open to the public than is usual on continental steamers, and one pleasing feature is a small working model of the engines which can be operated by steam.

For many years she was associated with the Vienna-Linz-Passau sailings, but in 1986 began a new venture, sailing on 2/3 day trips to Budapest. This was not entirely successful, and she has spent the summers since 1990 berthed at Budapest as a floating casino. Her operational future is very uncertain, although there has been a move to form a preservation group.

STADT WIEN & STADT PASSAU

Builders:	D.D.S.G., Werft Korneuburg, Vienna
Entered service:	STADT WIEN:1939, STADT PASSAU 1940
Length:	255 feet
Displacement:	650 tonnes
Passengers:	900 (54 in cabins)

These two ships have identical dimensions, and are virtually indistinguishable. It is said that they were built by specific order of Hitler after the annexation of Austria in 1938, and if so it would appear to have been one of his better decisions.

They have diesel-electric propulsion with the electric motors geared to the paddle shaft. Since there is no need for tall funnels which would inconveniently have to be lowered at each of the many bridges, each has a rather squat funnel and a hinged mast which is rarely seen in the upright position.

Apart from these features, they have a smart appearance and they are comfortably fitted out – *Stadt Wien* even has carpets in the engine room alleyways. They have overnight cabins for 54 passengers.

For almost their entire working lives they have been employed on the Vienna-Linz-Passau sailings, but on the cessation of this service in 1986 they were given new duties. *Stadt Passau* generally sails between Linz and Passau with occasional trips to Vienna, while *Stadt Wien* undertakes varied cruises from Vienna, sometimes to Bratislava in Slovakia.

To the southeast of Salzburg lies a mountainous region, called the Salzkammergut, where there are numerous small lakes, many of which have passenger services on them. The prosperity of the region is historically founded on the salt trade, and there are still salt mines in the area. Before roads and railways were built, the salt was transported on the lakes and rivers, eventually reaching the Danube.

With the advent of steam power, steamships were introduced on several of the lakes by the Englishmen Ruston and Andrews who in 1837 obtained the rights to provide services on all the lakes in Upper Austria. After the railways were built, the emphasis shifted to recreation and tourism. One of paddler from this era remains in steam, the superb *Gisela* of 1872 on the Traunsee, recently renovated and hopefully with a secure future. Another paddler, also dating from 1872, is still sailing but now converted to diesel power, the *Kaiser Franz Josef I* on the Wolfgangsee. At least three former screw steamers remain in service, although converted to diesel some time ago – on the Wolfgangsee there is *Elisabeth* (still sometimes referred to as *Kaiserin Elisabeth*), built for local ferry services in Budapest in 1873, *Helene* of 1887 on the nearby Mondsee and *Rudolf* (1903) on the Grundlsee.

Further afield, *Thalia*, a 127-foot screw steamer dating from 1909, has recently been restored to service on the Wörthersee. The small 80-passenger motor vessel *Grünberg* on the Traunsee has an unusual claim to fame. Built in 1926 for service on Bavaria's Starnbergersee, she was specially rebuilt in 1972 as a small paddle steamer *Tristan* for the film "Ludwig". The same footage also appeared in the film "Wagner", which had short appearances by *Kaiser Franz Josef I* and Lake Lucerne's *Schiller*.

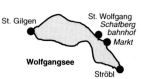

The Wolfgangsee is about 20 miles from Salzburg, the journey by postal coach taking just under an hour. The principal resorts are St. Gilgen at the western end and St. Wolfgang on the northern shore. A cogwheel railway, mainly steam-operated, runs from St. Wolfgang to the summit of the Schafberg, and a cable car scales the Zwölferhorn from St. Gilgen. The operetta "White Horse Inn" is set in St. Wolfgang, and the Inn itself ("Weisses Rössl" in German) is a prominent building beside the landing stage. This very picturesque resort recently celebrated its 1000th anniversary.

In summer there are 10 sailings daily by motor vessel running the full length of the lake from St. Gilgen to Ströbl with intermediate calls. In addition, *Elisabeth* and *Kaiser Franz Josef I* provide 3 and 8 sailings respectively between St. Gilgen and St. Wolfgang, the latter being an express service.

The Traunsee, 20 miles from the Wolfgangsee, is also a most attractive spot. It is dominated by the huge mass of the Traunstein, a mountain on the eastern shore which presents an almost sheer face towards the Lake.

From Ebensee, at the southern end of the Lake, a cable car climbs the nearby Feuerkogel mountain. The main resort is the charming little town of Gmunden at the northern extremity of the Lake. It is easily reached by rail from the main Salzburg-Vienna main line, one branch coming from Attnang-Puchheim and another from Lambach.

KAISER FRANZ JOSEF I

Builders:	Mayer, Linz
Entered service:	1872
Converted to diesel:	1954
Length:	110 feet
Displacement:	46·4 tonnes
Passengers:	250

This beautiful little paddler celebrated her centenary in 1972. By this time, however, she had already lost her steam engine and acquired a diesel motor geared on to the paddle shaft.

She is owned by Austrian Railways, rather surprisingly since no railway runs to the Lake. However, in former times there was a rail link, the Salzkammergut Lokalbahn, from Salzburg to Bad Ischl, and this explains the ownership of not only the *Kaiser* but also of the steam cogwheel railway up the Schafberg.

GISELA

Builders:	John Ruston, Vienna
Engines:	Ruston Foundry, Prague
Launched:	June 1871
Entered service:	Spring 1872
Length overall:	171 feet
Displacement:	135 tonnes
Speed:	11·9 knots
Passengers:	300 (formerly 501)

Although *Gisela*'s boiler was renewed in 1975, she is still coal-fired and retains her original two-cylinder oscillating engine which was built at Ruston's foundry in Prague in 1870. She was withdrawn in 1979, but a preservation movement was started locally. Ownership was transferred to the "Friends of Gmunden" as this gave financial advantages, and she was protected by being declared a National Monument – the first ship to be given this status. Renovation took several years, and she re-entered service on 5th July 1986. She now has a foremast and a small saloon aft which incorporates a Post Office.

Gisela was the last paddle steamer built for the Traunsee. Until the completion of the railway along the lakeside in 1877, the Austrian Emperor Franz Josef travelled on the lake steamers on the way to and from his holiday villa at Bad Ischl. In her early years *Gisela* had the honour of conveying him. The little steamer was named after his daughter.

Another paddler on the lake survived until quite recently – the *Elisabeth* of 1858. Unfortunately her hull and boiler did not pass an inspection in October 1967, and she was scrapped two years later. Her bridge telegraphs, made by Steven & Struthers in Glasgow, were transferred to *Gisela* during her major refit.

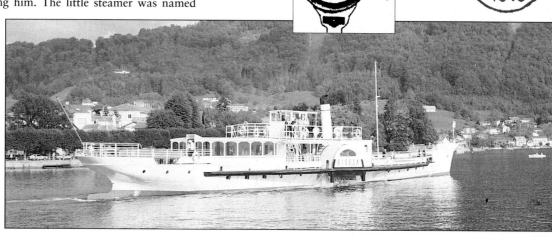

The most southeasterly province of West Germany is the formerly independent kingdom of Bavaria (Bayern in German) with its capital at Munich (München). The border with Austria runs through the Alps, and so several of the mountain lakes are in Bavaria. Paddle vessels, unfortunately both "dieselised", operate on two of the lakes, the Ammersee to the southwest of Munich and the Chiemsee to the southeast.

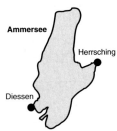

The Ammersee lies just to the north of the Alps, surrounded by low hills. It is a small lake, and would be undistinguished were it not for the presence of the paddler *Diessen*, dating from 1908. A sister ship, *Andechs*, which sailed from 1907 till 1955, survives as a houseboat but without engines and boiler. The main centre for Ammersee services, Herrsching, can easily be reached in 45 minutes by suburban railway from Munich (route S5).

The Chiemsee is on the direct route between Munich and Salzburg, 60 miles from the former and 40 from the latter. The lake is scenically attractive, with the Alps along the southern side, and several villages around the lakeside which are connected by an

intensive network of motor vessel services. The main railway line passes through Prien, which is therefore the focus of these services. From Prien station to the harbour at Prien-Stock is a distance of over a mile, but a metre gauge railway runs between the two. Many of the

services on this line are hauled by an amazing steam locomotive which was built in 1887. It gives the impression of being disguised as an ordinary carriage, with the chimney protruding from the roof, but the boiler is clearly visible inside. A ride on this delightful conveyance is essential for anyone visiting the Lake.

The main attractions are the two islands: Fraueninsel has a historic abbey and a fishing village, but it is the stunning Herrenchiemsee Castle on Herreninsel which is the most outstanding feature. Built to the design of the eccentric King Ludwig II as recently as 1885, it was modelled on Versailles, but it is in many ways even grander than the original.

All the ships in the Ludwig Fessler fleet are kept busy ferrying visitors to and from the islands. The larger vessels, including P.V. *Ludwig Fessler* operate sailings which call only at Prien, Gstadt and the two islands, but smaller motor vessels serve the outlying villages scattered round the shores of the Lake.

The Chiemsee-bahn outside Prien-stock station. The locomotive is nearest the camera.

DIESSEN

Builders:	J.A. Maffei, Munich
Entered service:	1908
Converted:	1974/75
Length:	125 feet
Passengers:	360

Diessen was coal-fired, with a compound diagonal engine, until 1974. During the following winter this was removed and replaced by a diesel-hydraulic system, that is, a diesel engine with the power transmitted to the paddle shaft by hydraulic means. Her paddle wheels have the unusual feature that they can be operated independently, giving her remarkable manoeuvrability.

Since re-entering service in 1975 she has been used on weekdays as well as Sundays, in contrast to her last few years with steam power. She provides ferry services on the lake, and there is no attempt to market her as a special attraction, or to put her on any kind of excursion sailings. She is, however, a very interesting little vessel, and it is well worth taking the trouble to sail on her.

Chiemseeschiffahrt
Ludwig Feßler

LUDWIG FESSLER

Builders:	Hitzler, Regensburg
Engines made by:	J.A. Maffei, Munich
Launched:	8th September 1926
Entered service:	12th April 1927
Converted to diesel	1972–73
Length overall:	174 feet
Speed:	11 knots
Passengers:	685

Ludwig Fessler, named after the founder of the operating company, is the last remaining paddler on the Lake. Her consort *Luitpold* was withdrawn in 1969 and three years later *Ludwig Fessler* was converted to diesel-hydraulic drive.

Her saloon is very elegant, decorated in turquoise with gold embellishments. The diesel motors are very well insulated, and she is a very pleasant little ship to travel on.

She sails daily in summer on a service from Prien-Stock, visiting the islands of Fraueninsel and Herreninsel.

The deepest of the north Italian lakes, Lake Como is famous for its dreamy lakeside villas, the most renowned being the Villa Carlotta at Cadenabbia on the western shore. From its azalea-filled gardens there are fine views across the lake to Bellagio, on the extreme end of the promontory which divides the lake, as well as the more distant Grigna mountains rising to over 8000 feet.

The lake is served by the Navigazione Sul Lago Di Como (NLC) fleet of seven hydrofoils, fourteen motor vessels and two paddle steamers; car ferries link Cadenabbia with Bellagio and Varenna. The principal route is from Como north to Colico, while the arm of the lake to Lecco receives only about four services per day.

Moored at Colico since 1970 is the paddle steamer *Plinio*, now used as a yacht club and bar-restaurant. Her engines and boiler have been removed but externally she is little changed since she was last in service over a quarter of a century ago.

Another interesting vessel is the motorship *Milano*, built as a paddle steamer in 1895 and converted in 1950. She retains a tall funnel and sponsons, and it is only her wash which betrays her secret when she is under way.

Only the northern tip of Lake Maggiore lies in Switzerland, the major part stretching some thirty miles into Italy. From resorts such as Stresa and Pallanza it is a short boat trip to the area's greatest attraction – the Borromean Islands. Isola Pescatori is like a

fisherman's village, Isola Madre is almost entirely occupied by botanical gardens while the best known, Isola Bella, has a magnificent palace and formal gardens.

The lake steamers are operated by Navigazione Lago Maggiore (NLM), an Italian company based in Arona. There are local sailings centred on the Swiss resort of Locarno as well as extensive services in the Italian section, but very few sailings traverse the entire length of the lake – less than 5% of the company's passengers make a "cross-frontier" cruise.

Garda is the largest of the Italian lakes, being 32 miles long and 10 miles across. The southern end is bounded by vineyards and groves of orange. lemon and olive trees, all thriving in the mild Mediterranean climate. Further north, the lake is deeper and narrower, giving a fjord-like appearance to the scenery. Regular motor vessel and hydrofoil services link popular resorts such as Garda, Limone and Riva – a charming old town with its waterfront dominated by the 12th century La Rocca castle.

PATRIA (ex SAVOIA)

Builders:	N. Odero, Genoa
Entered service:	1926
Length:	172 feet
Displacement:	286 tonnes
Passengers:	900

Patria and her sister *Concordia* are half-saloon steamers kept in immaculate condition despite their limited use. They appear to be treated as normal units of the fleet and their sailings are not given any special prominence in the timetable.

In 1983 *Patria* was given a tall black funnel with one white ring, replacing the previous squat funnel fitted when she was converted to oil burning some thirty years previously. Her wood-panelled lower saloon is most elegant and even the engine-room alleyway has leather armchairs from which it is possible to view the paddlewheels through large glass windows.

In 1990 *Patria* offered a dance cruise from Lecco on Saturday nights. There then followed a Sunday morning departure for a four hour cruise to the centre of the Lake.

During that season it became known that her owners were considering withdrawing *Patria* at the end of it. By 1994 no decision had yet been taken on her future, conversion to diesel power being a real possibility. Attempts are being made to persuade the NLC to recognise her tourist potential and keep her in steam.

CONCORDIA sails light from the Tavernola shipyard to her berth at Como.

CONCORDIA (ex XXVIII OTTOBRE)

Builders:	N. Odero, Genoa
Entered service:	1927
Length:	172 feet
Displacement:	294 tonnes
Passengers:	900

Concordia began life as the *XXVIII Ottobre* this unique name commemorating Mussolini's march to Rome on 28th October 1922. Her present name dates from 1943 and, like *Patria*, she retains her original triple expansion diagonal steam machinery. She underwent a major refit from 1973 to 1977 during which time she received new wheelhouse, boiler and an additional saloon on top of he original half saloon. This latter structure together with her two white funnel rings makes her easily distinguishable from *Patria*. The extra enclosed accommodation is fitted out as a restaurant which makes her ideally suited for lunch-inclusive cruises.

She spends most of the week lying at the Tavernola shipyard, but on Sundays she leaves Como shortly before noon for the seven hour round trip to Colico. If you wish lunch it is advisable to book well in advance as this sailing attracts large numbers of hungry (and noisy!) Italians.

These two lovely steamers are full of Italian atmosphere and are well worth a visit.

PIEMONTE (ex REGINA MADRE)

Builders:	Escher-Wyss, Zürich
Entered service:	1904
Length:	168 feet
Displacement:	273 tonnes
Passengers:	500

Piemonte, now the only paddle steamer operating on Lake Maggiore, underwent a major refit from 1961 to 1965 and again in 1973-74 when she received a new boiler. In the late 'seventies she operated lunch cruises from Locarno and Ascona, and gained an international audience of millions when she appeared in television commercials for Martini. Nowadays she enjoys a very cosseted existence, sailing only on a handful of evening cruises in mid-August and occasional charters. These rare outings resulted in her carrying a total of 3118 passengers in 1988, for example.

For the past few years she has sailed for a few days in October on short cruises from Locarno, in the Swiss sector of the lake. In 1993 it was impossible to operate these due to flooding, as the landing stages were under several feet of water.

A former consort, the paddle steamer *Lombardia* (1904-1958), is still in existence as a restaurant and night-club in Arona harbour.

G. ZANARDELLI

Builders:	Escher-Wyss, Zürich
Entered service:	1903
Converted to diesel:	1976
Length:	160 feet
Displacement:	215 tonnes
Passengers:	500

Zanardelli, at one time known as *Giuseppe Zanardelli*, is the elder of the two remaining paddle steamers on Lake Garda. She is named after a notable Prime Minister of Italy (1901-1903) who came from the nearby town of Brescia. In 1944 she was damaged in an aerial attack near Limone, fatalities being recorded. She was in regular service throughout the fifties but the following decade saw her laid up. She underwent major internal revision including the fitting of a glassed-in upper deck saloon before resuming employment in 1969.

Zanardelli was badly damaged in October 1977 after grounding on a ledge of rocks while on an early morning sailing. It was six years before she returned to service and was now powered by diesel-hydraulic machinery. She is well maintained but in recent years she appears to have been used only for charters and spends most of her time in the shipyard at Peschiera.

ITALIA

Builders:	N. Odero, Genoa
Entered service:	1909
Converted to diesel:	1977
Length:	160 feet
Displacement:	252 tonnes
Passengers:	600

Like her elder sister, *Italia* did not emerge unscathed from World War II; in 1945, while serving as a German hospital ship, she was bombed and sunk off Sirmione, not returning to service until 1952. In 1970 she was fitted with a modern wheelhouse and a glassed-in upper saloon which encloses the lower half of her funnel. She did not sail in 1975 or 1976 but returned the following season with new diesel-hydraulic machinery in place of her original steam engines. Most unusually, *Italia* and *Zanardelli* have independent paddles and, as a result, are highly manoeuvrable.

From mid-July until mid-September, *Italia* is employed five afternoons a week on popular round-the-lake cruises. An attractive multi-lingual handbill showed her 1992 departure points as Peschiera on Mondays, Salò on Tuesdays, Riva on Wednesdays, Desenzano on Thursdays and Garda on Fridays. Each day had several other pick-ups and the standard fare for the cruise was 20,000 lire (about £10). There was also a late-night cruise from Desenzano and Sirmione on Saturdays in August.